THE FACTS OF ACTS

HAZEL JAYCOX BROWN

Abingdon Press / Nashville

Library of Congress Cataloging–in–Publication Data

Brown, Hazel Jaycox.
   The facts of Acts / Hazel Jaycox Brown.
      p.   cm.
   ISBN 0-687-00277-X (alk. paper)
    1. Bible. N.T. Acts—Miscellanea. 2. Bible games and puzzles.
I. Title.
BS2625.5.B76   1995
226.6'007—dc20   94–47500
                                            CIP

95 96 97 98 99 00 01 02 03 04 — 10 9 8 7 6 5 4 3 2 1

MANUFACTURED IN THE UNITED STATES OF AMERICA

Acknowledgments

1. I am grateful to these precious folks who helped obtain the different languages for the quiz, "Nominees for Best Foreign Language"

> Anneva Sander and her mother, Martha Schoenhals—German
> Shelly and Israel Palacios—Spanish
> Ramona and James Redinger—Hebrew
> Connie Young, missionary to Rwanda—Kinyarwanda
> Marvin and Vickie Garrison—Swedish
> Keith Brown, our son who lives in Athens, Greece—French, Ancient Greek, Modern Greek

2. My indebtedness to David, my excellent at-home editor, collaborator, and dear husband, never ends.

3. My appreciation of my prayer partners and women's Bible study group grows daily.

4. My deep gratitude goes to Marvin Cropsey, my editor, for his special interest and work in behalf of these books, as well as to others at Abingdon who work on these projects.

5. Most of all, I thank and praise my wonderful Savior and Lord for providing His marvelous Word of Life, which when studied daily brings light, insight, and delight to my soul.

Preface

Have you ever noted that *SWORD* is *WORD* with an S in front of it? In Ephesians 6 the sword is mentioned as part of the full armor of God that we are to put on (vv. 11, 13). Verse 17 says that the "Sword of the Spirit is the Word of God."

Swords get dull at times, and to be effective they must be sharpened. These Bible puzzles and quizzes are a way to sharpen your Sword and your mind.

Scriptures in this book are taken from the New International Version unless otherwise noted. Helpful references are included in most activities, so feel free to use your Bible. Many of these puzzles and quizzes are in reality mini-Bible studies. They will teach, refresh your memories, and serve as good mind-reinforcers. You will sharpen your mind and learn more about God from His Word. Wonderful growth will take place.

Read the Scripture at the beginning again. That is a promise. We will be ever bearing fresh fruit as we study and live by God's Word. God isn't finished with us yet. He has wonderful plans as we follow Him.

Gentlemen, women, are you ready?
BEGIN! SHARPEN YOUR SWORDS!

Contents

CAST OF CHARACTERS

All the names of the characters are separated into letter combinations. Reassemble them for the answers. The first one is done for you.

A, AG, AGA, ~~ANA~~, APO, AQU, ~~AS~~, BA, BAS, BUS

CH, CRI, DEM, ER, ET, EU, FE, HER, HN, HY

IL, JO, LAS, LIX, LL, LLA, MA ~~NI~~, OD, OS

OT, PA, PET, PRI, RI, RIP, RK, RNA, SCI, SI

SP, TIM, TY, US, US, US

1. Went to counsel Saul in Damascus. (9:10-19) <u>A N A N I A S</u>

2. Preached sermon: 3,000 converted. (2:14-41) _ _ _ _ _ _

3. Teamed with Paul on the first missionary journey. (13:2-3) _ _ _ _ _ _ _ _

4. Young man deserting missionary team. (15:36-39) _ _ _ _ _ _ _ _ _

5. Paul's primary second and third missionary journey partner. (15:40) _ _ _ _ _ _

6. Young man who became coworker and "son in the faith" to Paul. (16:1-3) _ _ _ _ _ _ _ _

7. Fellow tentmakers and ministers of the gospel with Paul. (18:2, 3) _ _ _ _ _ _ _ _ _ _ _ _ _ _

8. Corinth synagogue ruler who became a Christian. (18:8) _ _ _ _ _ _ _

9. The eloquent Alexandrian needing more instruction in the gospel. (18:24-26) _ _ _ _ _ _ _

10. The angry silversmith at Ephesus. (19:24-31) _ _ _ _ _ _ _ _

11. Fell asleep and out a window during Paul's long sermon. (20:9-10) _ _ _ _ _ _ _ _ _

12. Prophesied at Caesarea that the wearer of
    "this belt" would be handed over to the
    Gentiles. (21:10-11)   _ _ _ _ _ _

13. Struck dead by an angel of the Lord because
    he failed to praise God. (12:22-23)   _ _ _ _ _ _

14. First Caesarean governor to hear Paul's
    testimony. (24)   _ _ _ _ _

15. Festus consults with this king before sending
    Paul to Rome. (25, 26)   _ _ _ _ _ _ _

SETTING THE SCENE

_____ 1. Place where disciples were first called Christians. (11:26)

_____ 2. Barnabas and John Mark headed here without Paul. (15:39)

_____ 3. Crippled beggar was healed by Peter. (3:1-10)

_____ 4. The gospel is declared to be for the Gentiles at Cornelius' house located in this city. (10:23-48)

_____ 5. Peter explains here why he entered a Gentile home. (11:1-18)

_____ 6. The initial giving of the Holy Spirit to followers of Christ was here. (1:12–2:4)

_____ 7. Paul spent three years there, warning them day and night with tears. (20:17-31)

_____ 8. Saul's home town. (9:11).

_____ 9. Paul and Silas imprisoned there; after worship and singing, there was an earthquake. (16:12-34)

_____ 10. Place of prayer meeting for Peter, who was imprisoned. God sent His angel to release him. (12:5-14)

_____ 11. Death site of Judas Iscariot. (1:18, 19)

_____ 12. After great persecution broke out against the church at Jerusalem, Philip went to this area to preach. (8:4-8)

a. Tarsus

b. Upper Room in Jerusalem

c. Akeldama

d. Temple Gate, Beautiful

e. Jerusalem

f. House of Mary, John Mark's mother

g. Cyprus

h. Ephesus

i. Philippi

j. Samaria

k. Caesarea

l. Antioch

OPENING ACTS
(Acts 1–4)

Below are two groups of events recorded in Acts, which are out of order. Put each group in correct *order as recorded in Scripture*. You may need your Bible. Place sequence numeral on line before event.

I. CHAPTERS 1 AND 2 (NUMBER 1 TO 10)

______ Ascension of Jesus.

______ Mathias chosen as apostle.

______ Fate of Judas described.

______ Believers, including Jesus' mother, gather to pray and to choose replacement for Judas Iscariot.

______ Peter preaches a powerful sermon.

______ Jews speaking different languages could understand one another.

______ Sound of a violent wind fills house.

______ 3,000 saved.

______ Appearance of tongues of fire resting on each head.

______ Promise of the Holy Spirit.

II. CHAPTERS 3 AND 4 (NUMBER 1 TO 7)

______ A strong unity between believers; shares possessions.

______ Peter and John appear before Sanhedrin.

______ Barnabas sold possessions and brought the money before the apostles.

______ Peter and John arrested.

______ Peter and John ordered not to speak or teach in the name of Jesus.

______ Peter preaches repentance to onlookers.

______ Peter heals the crippled beggar.

WHO ACTED THIS WAY?

Use the sets of letters below to help you find *WHO,* and to fill the lines after each numbered statement. All will be used once.

AN,   AN,   AN,   AS,   BAR   BAS,   CAS,   CER   COR,   DOR

EL,   ER,   ETH,   EUN,   GA,   HN,   IAS,   IO,   IRA,   JA

JE,   JO,   KE,   LI,   LI,   LIP,   LU,   MA,   MAT,   MES

MON,   NA,   NE,   PE,   PH,   PHEN,   PHI,   PI,   SA,   SAP

SI,   SOR,   STE,   SUS,   TER,   THI,   UCH,   UL,   US

1. Two unschooled, ordinary men
   who did extraordinary things. (chap. 4)   — — — — —

2. Two who sold property, conspired
   together, lied, then died   — — — — —
   separately. (chap. 5)   — — — — — — — —

3. A highly respected teacher
   of the law, told the Sanhedrin to
   leave Peter and John alone. (chap. 5)   — — — — — — —

4. Proclaimed Christ in Samaria.
   (chap. 8)   — — — — — —

5. Instructed the disciples to
   wait for the GIFT. (chap. 1)   — — — — —

6. Accused of blasphemy, stoned
   to death. (chap. 7)   — — — — — —

7. Tried buying gift of the
   laying on of hands to receive   — — — — — the
   the Holy Spirit. (chap. 8)   — — — — — — —

8. Set out to destroy the church, dragging
   Christians off to prison. (chap. 9)   — — — —

9. Philip explained a passage
   from Isaiah to this man. (chap. 8)   — — — — — — — — — —
                                          — — — — — — —

10. Chosen to replace Judas Iscariot
    as one of the Twelve. (chap. 1)   — — — — — — — — —

11. Gentile centurion seeking
    help from Peter. (chap. 10)   — — — — — — — — —

12. Name means son of
    encouragement or consolation. (chap. 4)   — — — — — — — —

13. This lady was raised from
    the dead. (chap. 9)   — — — — — — —

14. Christian martyr, brother
    of John. (chap. 12)   — — — — — —

15. Writer of the book of Acts. (1:1;
    Luke 1:3, note word "we" in
    Acts 16:10-17 and 2 Tim. 4:11)   — — — — —

SCENE CHANGES

_____ 1. Paul testified before Gov. Felix here. (24)	a. Athens
_____ 2. Jesus ascended here. (1:10-12)	b. Perga in Pamphylia
_____ 3. Jesus confronts Saul on the _____ road. (9:3-6)	c. Joppa
_____ 4. Shipwrecked, prisoner Paul lands here. (28:1)	d. Caesarea
_____ 5. Paul explains who the "unknown God" is. (17:16-31)	e. Mount of Olives
_____ 6. Where John Mark deserted Paul and Barnabas. (13:13)	f. Council at Jerusalem
_____ 7. Paul lives in house under guard, but able to preach. (28:16, 30, 31)	g. Lystra
_____ 8. Where Peter raised Dorcas (Tabitha) from the dead. (9:36-43)	h. Temple in Jerusalem
_____ 9. Paul stoned, left for dead. (14:8-20)	i. Malta
_____10. Gentile code of Christian living established here. (15:1-29)	j. Rome
_____11. Paul dragged out, about to be stoned, but Roman soldiers intervene. (21:27-32)	k. Damascus

WHAT COMES NEXT?
(Acts 5–8)

Below are two groups of events recorded in Acts, which are out of order. Put each group in correct order as recorded in Scripture by placing numerals on the lines in order or sequence. Feel free to use your Bible.

I. CHAPTER 5 (NUMBER 1 TO 10)

______ Peter said, "We must obey God rather than man."

______ Apostles rejoice to suffer for His Name.

______ Ananias and Sapphira lie and die.

______ Many healings performed by apostles.

______ Apostles sent to preach at temple courts.

______ Apostles flogged and ordered not to speak Jesus' name.

______ Angel of the Lord opened the doors of the jail.

______ Apostles brought before the Sanhedrin.

______ Gamaliel says if their activity is human, it will die; if of God, no one can stop it.

______ Apostles jailed.

II. CHAPTERS 6, 7, 8 (NUMBER 1 TO 12)

______ Philip preaches in Samaria.

______ Stephen's face like that of an angel's.

______ Seven chosen as deacons.

______ Stephen dies from stoning.

______ Philip taken away by the Spirit of the Lord.

______ Stephen speaks to Sanhedrin.

______ Saul first appears in Scripture.

______ Persecution severe, Christians scatter.

______ Stephen looks up and sees Jesus.

______ Simon the Sorcerer seeks Holy Spirit with money.

______ Stephen accused of blasphemy.

______ Ethiopian eunuch converted.

KEEPING
THE CHARACTERS STRAIGHT

Fill in the blanks below and then find the names in the word search. You will need help with the spelling of some names. Use the references to Acts as needed.

PEOPLE OF ACTS BY NAME

A _ _ _ _ (4:6), high priest

A _ _ _ _ _ (1:13), apostle

C _ _ _ _ _ (25:8), ruler

C _ _ _ _ _ _ (18:8), synagogue leader

D _ _ _ _ _ _ _ (24:24), Felix's wife

D _ _ _ _ _ _ _ _ (19:24), silversmith

E _ _ _ _ _ _ (19:22), Paul's helper

G _ _ _ _ _ _ _ (5:34), teacher of the law

J _ _ _ _ (12:2), first martyred apostle

C _ _ _ _ _ _ _ _ L _ _ _ _ _ (23:26), Roman commander

J _ _ _ _ (1:13), son of Alphaeus, apostle

J _ _ _ _ (1:13), son of James, apostle

J _ _ _ _ _ (1:23), called Barsabbas

M _ _ _ (12:12), mother of John Mark

N _ _ _ _ _ _ (6:5), one of the Seven

P _ _ _ _ _ (1:13), apostle

P _ _ _ _ _ _ (28:7), Malta estate owner

S _ _ _ _ (8:9), the sorcerer

T _ _ _ _ _ _ J _ _ _ _ _ _ (18:7), served God

T _ _ _ _ _ _ _ _ 20:4), accompanied Paul

T _ _ _ _ _ _ _ _ _ (24:1), lawyer

B _ _ _ _ _ _ (25:23), Agrippa's sister

C _ _ _ _ _ _ _ (4:6), high priest

C _ _ _ _ _ _ _ _ _ (10:1), Gentile

S _ _ _ _ _ _ P _ _ _ _ _ (13:7), proconsul

E _ _ _ _ _ (13:8), sorcerer

D _ _ _ _ _ _ _ _ (17:34), new believer

G _ _ _ _ _ (18:12), proconsul

J _ _ _ _ (15:22), called Barsabbas

J _ _ _ (1:5), baptized with water

S _ _ _ _ (1:13) the Zealot, apostle

M _ _ _ _ _ _ (13:1) Antioch church leader

L _ _ _ _ (16:14), sold purple cloth

N _ _ _ _ _ _ (6:5), one of the Seven

J _ _ _ M _ _ _ (12:25), went with Paul

L _ _ _ _ _ (13:1) a leader at Antioch

S _ _ _ _ _ _ _ (20:4), went with Paul

S _ _ _ _ _ (13:1) called Niger—Antioch

T _ _ _ _ (6:5), one of the Seven

P _ _ _ _ _ _ _ (6:5), one of the Seven

T _ _ _ _ _ _ _ _ (20:4), Paul's helper

PEOPLE IDENTIFIED BY OCCUPATION ONLY   *OLD TESTAMENT MEN MENTIONED*

c _ _ _ _ _ _ o _ t _ _ _ _ _ g _ _ _ _ (5:24)   I _ _ _ _ _ (8:28)

s _ _ _ _ g _ _ _, f _ _ _ _ _ _ _ t _ _ _ _ _ _ (16:16)   J _ _ _ _ _ _ (7:45)

c _ _ _ _ _ _ _ _ b _ _ <u>g</u> <u>a</u> <u>r</u> (3:2)   A _ _ _ _ (7:40)

P _ _ _ _ _ _ _ _ _ _ _ j _ _ _ _ _ (16:12, 23)   I _ _ _ _ (3:13)

c _ _ _ _ _ _ _ _ _ _ (23:23)   J _ _ _ _ (7:32)

c _ _ _ _ _ _ _ _ (21:31)   A _ _ _ _ _ _ (7:8)

m _ _ _ _ _ _ _ _ _ _ _ (16:20)   M _ _ _ _ (3:22)

s _ _ _ _ _ _ _ (12:6)   D _ _ _ _ (1:16)

s _ _ _ _ _ _ _ _ (12:4)   J _ _ _ (2:16)

c _ _ _ _ p _ _ _ _ _ _ (25:15)

```
C O T R O P H I M U S E C U N D U S T H E R L
L P E O L E H P G A M A L I E L Y M A S I C C
A I N E M A G I S T R A T E S L U C I U S R R
U A O C N T S S L A D Y E R A S T U S B E I I
D J E O F A I J K I L A L L I S U R D L C P P
I G M H A N S O U Q P S T R N S P M L P A P P
U I S C V J U D A S E P K O W X C E Y U B L L
S A E A O F I Z M S D R I K R L T G H B R E E
L I R I J B L J O N A R O A H E T S T L A D D
Y P G A A B E M R M U S S S N B O S E I H B B
S S I P M O N Y N T U E U U E J U C R U A E E
I T U H E C R H N I A T T O V N A R T S M G G
A S S A S A O E R C S R I N O B P I U E C G G
S E P S X J C T F U O L O E A I S S L M H A A
D I A N D R E W J F L M M E L A G P L E I R R
N R U O M M S S L A I I M I I K R U U J R D D
S P L P E E U R G T S Q H A R S T S S U J I I
R F U D M I I J O S E P H W N X Y V N E D O O
E E S A T G B M A N A E N L Y D I A O C I N N
I I J I E F P R O C O R U S G J E L R I V Y Y
D H T V S A D U J N I C A N O R K R A N A S S
L C A P T A I N O F T E M P L E G U A R D I I
O L E R Q T Y C H I C U S I M O N P M E N U U
S E N T R I E S N I C O L A S A N N A B O S S
```

HOLY SPIRIT SPECIAL EFFECTS

The book of Acts tells of six occasions when the gift of the Holy Spirit was given. Here, choose the number(s) from the appropriate list of possible answers on the following pages for each of those times. Follow Scripture passages carefully. Use some numbers more than once; others not at all.

A. Acts 2:1-41 (also 1:12-15)

_______ Who?

_______ When?

_______ Where?

_______ Why meet?

_______ Sound heard?

_______ Seen?

_______ Felt?

_______ Tongues?

_______ Results mentioned?

____

____

____

B. Acts 4:23-33

_______ Who?

_______ When?

_______ Where?

_______ Why meet?

_______ Sound heard?

_______ Seen?

_______ Felt?

_______ Tongues?

_______ Results?

____

____

____

C. Acts 8:4-25

_______ Who?

_______ When?

_______ Where?

_______ Why meet?

_______ Sound heard?

_______ Seen?

_______ Felt?

_______ Tongues?

_______ Results?

____

____

____

D. Acts 9:3-20

_______ Who?

_______ When?

_______ Where?

_______ Why meet?

_______ Felt?

_______ Tongues?

_______ Results?

____

____

E. Acts 10:24-48

_______ Who?

_______ When?

_______ Where?

_______ Why meet?

_______ Felt?

_______ Tongues?

_______ Results?

____

____

F. Acts 19:1-7

_______ Who?

_______ When?

_______ Where?

_______ Why meet?

_______ Felt?

_______ Tongues?

_______ Results?

____

____

CHOOSE ANSWERS FROM THE APPROPRIATE LISTS BELOW:

Who?

1. Peter and John with others
2. Ananias and Sapphira
3. About 120 of Jesus' followers
4. Paul with believers
5. Ananias with Saul
6. Peter with Cornelius and others
7. Not mentioned in passage
8. Paul with Lydia and others

Where?

21. At Caesarea in his home
22. Not mentioned in passage
23. Ephesus
24. Damascus
25. Samaria
26. Upper Room in Jerusalem
27. In Joppa
28. Back with their own people

Heard?

41. Not mentioned in passage
42. A blowing, violent wind sound filled house
43. A voice from heaven

Seen?

51. Not mentioned in passage
52. Something like tongues of fire that separated and rested on each one
53. A dove dropped down from the sky

When?

11. After Jesus confronts Saul
12. After release from Sanhedrin Court
13. After Philip preached there
14. After shipwreck
15. After visions from the Lord
16. At Council in Jerusalem
17. On third missionary journey
18. On day of Pentecost
19. Not mentioned in passage

Why meet?

31. Special prayer for boldness to obey despite threats
32. Prayer
33. To decide certain issues
34. So the Holy Spirit would come on believers there
35. Not mentioned in passage
36. God had told him to meet with this man

Felt?

61. Not mentioned in passage
62. Hands laid on
63. Warmth flowing through body
64. Place shaken

Tongues?

71. Not mentioned in Scripture
72. Spoke in other tongues—languages

Results Mentioned?

81. Not mentioned in passage
82. They prophesied
83. They praised God
84. They preached boldly
85. They spoke the Word boldly
86. Crowd heard speaking, each in his or her own language
87. Unity
88. Shared possessions
89. 3,000 converted that day
90. Baptized in the name of Jesus
91. Simon the sorcerer tried to buy the ability
92. Other Samaritan villages heard the gospel
93. Started preaching about Jesus
94. Holy Spirit given to Gentiles as well as Jews
95. Sight restored
96. Peter spoke powerfully to large crowd

KNOW YOUR SCRIPT
(Acts 1–14)

Using your Bible, go through the chapters in Acts to find where these events took place. Or maybe you know the book well enough to try it without using the Bible. Write the number of the chapters before the statement.

______   1. Peter raised Dorcas (Tabitha) from the dead.

______   2. The choosing of the Seven.

______   3. Mathias chosen to take Judas Iscariot's place.

______   4. Peter heals the man crippled from birth.

______   5. The initial coming of the Holy Spirit.

______   6. Disciples first called Christians.

______ – ______   7. First missionary journey chapters.

______   8. The ascension of Jesus.

______   9. Peter's first big successful evangelistic meeting—3,000 saved.

______ 10. Saul's conversion.

______ 11. Steven stoned, first Christian martyr.

______ 12. Philip instructs the Ethiopian eunuch.

______, ______ 13. Two miraculous escapes from prison by Peter.

______ 14. The Holy Spirit given to the Gentiles initially, Cornelius and household.

______ 15. First mention of Saul in Acts.

______ 16. Ananias and Sapphira lie and die, one at a time.

FOLLOW YOUR SCRIPT, PLEASE
(Acts 15–28)

Using your Bible, go through the chapters in Acts to find where these events took place. Or maybe you know the book well enough to try it without using the Bible. Write the number of the chapter(s) before the statement.

______   1. Paul's time in Rome.

______   2. Aquila and Priscilla join in evangelism.

______   3. Prisoner Paul and others shipwrecked.

______ – ______   4. Paul's third missionary journey chapters.

______   5. Council at Jerusalem.

______   6. Paul arrested at Jerusalem.

______   7. Apollos joins in evangelism.

______ – ______   8. Second missionary journey chapters.

______   9. Paul's and Silas's shackles broken; Philippian jailer believes.

______   10. Lydia converted.

______   11. Paul's testimony before Felix.

______   12. Paul and others safe on the island of Malta.

______   13. Paul's trial before Festus.

______, ______   14. Paul's testimony before King Agrippa.

______   15. Paul's vision of the man of Macedonia.

CROSSING THE STAGE

References after clues are from the book of Acts.

ACROSS

4. The Jews asked this leader to execute Jesus. (13:26-28)
6. The Jews brought charges against Paul in front of this governor. (ch. 24)
8. Prophet who warned Paul about imprisonment in Jerusalem. (21:10, 11)
9. A synagogue ruler whom the Jews turned against. (18:17)
11. A paralytic healed in the name of Jesus by Peter. (9:33-34)
13. Because of a vow, Paul had this done to his hair at Cenchrea. (18:18)
15. "Come over to Macedonia and _?_ us," a man in a vision told Paul. (16:9)
16. "Then how is it that each of us hears them in his own native _?_?" (2:8)
18. Girl who kept Peter waiting at the door after his escape from jail. (12:13-14)
20. One of the original disciples. (1:13)
22. A Thessalonian convert was Paul's host and got into trouble for it. (17:1-9)
24. Paul's traveling companion seized in the riot at Ephesus. (19:29)
25. Philip instructed this Ethiopian in the Scriptures. (8:26-39)
26. Ascended into heaven. (ch. 1)
27. As a Jew he was better known as Saul. (13:9)
28. Berean son of Pyrrhus—one who went with Paul to Jerusalem. (20:1-4)
29. Three men, same name: a liar, a disciple, and an unscrupulous high priest. (5:3; 9:10; 24:1)
31. The kind of charges made against Paul. (25:7)
32. Evangelist, one of the Seven, with four daughters who prophesied. (21:8, 9)
34. He wished that Paul hadn't already appealed to Caesar. (26:27-32)
35. Peter raised this lady from the dead. (9:36-41)
36. Cornelius said he was "praying at this _?_." (10:30)
37. ". . . heard that the Gentiles also had received the word of _?_." (11:1)

39. Selected to take Judas Iscariot's place as member of the Twelve. (1:23-26)

41. "An angel of the Lord opened the doors of the __?__ ." (5:19)

43. He tried to silence the mob at the riot in Ephesus. (19:33)

46. A word not found in Acts, but used to close prayers, meaning "so be it."

47. Queen of Ethiopia. (8:27)

48. One of the Twelve. (1:13)

49. Stephen told his accusers, "You always __?__ the Holy Spirit!" (7:51)

50. A man from Asia who accompanied Paul. (20:4)

51. "He came . . . to Lystra, where a disciple named Timothy _?_ " (16:1)

52. This lady became a follower under Paul's ministry. (17:34)

DOWN

1. One of the Twelve. (1:13)
2. Woman in Upper Room with disciples and others—waiting, praying. (1:14)
3. He died a horrible death in a field he had bought. (1:18-19)
4. He led Cornelius and other Gentiles to receive the Holy Spirit. (10:30-45)
5. He stayed with Silas at Berea while Paul went to the coast. (17:13-14)
6. He sought King Agrippa's opinion about Paul. (ch. 25–26)
7. Stephen used this character from Genesis to make a point in his defense. (7:9-18)
9. One of the Seven, stoned to death. (ch. 6–7)
10. Paul raised him from the dead. (20:7-10)
12. A Jewish chief priest, father of seven sons. (19:14)
14. *Beautiful* was the name of a temple _?_ . (3:2)
17. A trusted personal servant of King Herod. (12:20)
19. Priscilla and Aquila instructed this eloquent, learned man. (18:24-28)
21. To whom Luke writes this book. (1:1)
23. This Pharisee fell to the ground when a great light flashed. (9:3, 4)
26. He and Peter were jailed for preaching. (4:1-23)
27. Wife of Aquila. (18:2)
28. Wife who told the same lie as her husband, then died. (5:1-10)
29. A Thessalonian who accompanied Paul. (20:4)
30. Peter stayed at this tanner's home in Joppa. (9:43)
33. One of the Seven, mentioned only one time. (6:5)
38. His name means "Son of Encouragement." (4:36)
40. Accompanied Paul on the second missionary journey. (15:40)
42. Paul's close friend, coworker in ministry, and fellow tentmaker. (18:2-3)
44. Got Peter out of prison. (12:7-10)
45. King, who failed to give praise to God, was struck down, eaten by worms and died. (12:19-23)

THE PLOT THICKENS
(Acts 9–12)

Below are two groups of events recorded in Acts. Put each group in correct order as recorded in Scripture.

I. CHAPTERS 9 AND 10 (Number 1 to 13)

______ In a basket Saul escapes by being lowered from a hole in the wall.

______ Peter goes to Cornelius' house.

______ Jesus confronts Saul on Damascus Road.

______ God sends Ananias to Saul.

______ Saul starts trip to persecute Christians.

______ Peter raises Dorcas (Tabitha) from the dead.

______ Barnabas brings Saul to the Apostles.

______ Cornelius sends men to Joppa to get Peter.

______ Saul receives sight and Holy Spirit.

______ Peter learns what is clean and unclean.

______ The Holy Spirit first given to Gentiles.

______ Saul preaches in Damascus; life endangered.

______ Saul speaks boldly in Jerusalem; sent to Tarsus.

II. CHAPTERS 11 AND 12 (Number 1 to 9)

______ Barnabas and Saul minister in Antioch.

______ Peter defends actions concerning the Gentiles.

______ Herod suffers God's fatal judgment.

______ Barnabas and Saul return to Antioch with John Mark.

______ Peter appears at the door of a prayer meeting.

______ James, brother of John, martyred by Herod.

______ An angel frees Peter.

______ Many saved in Antioch under Barnabas.

______ Peter imprisoned.

MODUS OPERANDI

Whom did God use to perform supernatural feats in others? Choose one.

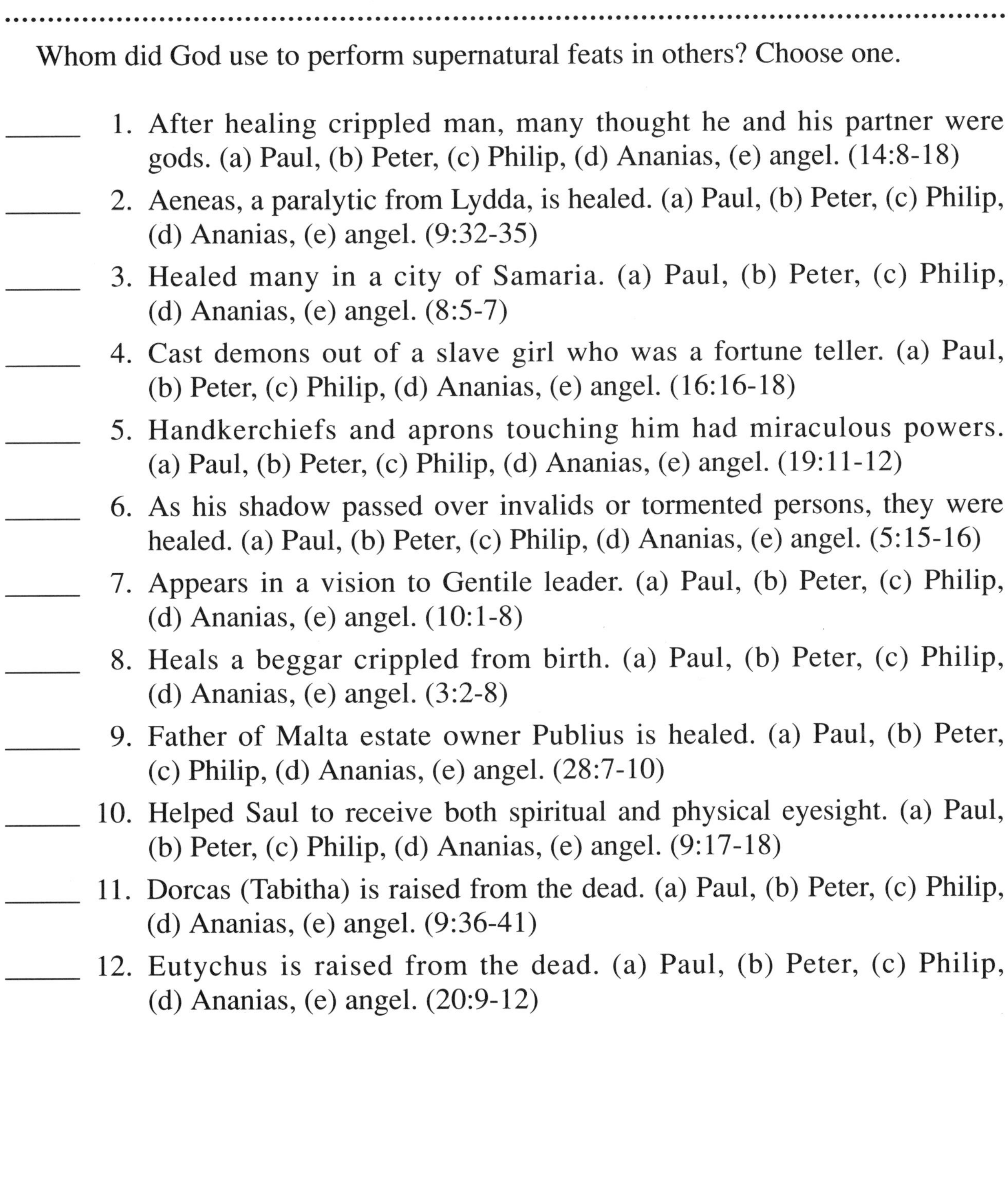

______ 1. After healing crippled man, many thought he and his partner were gods. (a) Paul, (b) Peter, (c) Philip, (d) Ananias, (e) angel. (14:8-18)

______ 2. Aeneas, a paralytic from Lydda, is healed. (a) Paul, (b) Peter, (c) Philip, (d) Ananias, (e) angel. (9:32-35)

______ 3. Healed many in a city of Samaria. (a) Paul, (b) Peter, (c) Philip, (d) Ananias, (e) angel. (8:5-7)

______ 4. Cast demons out of a slave girl who was a fortune teller. (a) Paul, (b) Peter, (c) Philip, (d) Ananias, (e) angel. (16:16-18)

______ 5. Handkerchiefs and aprons touching him had miraculous powers. (a) Paul, (b) Peter, (c) Philip, (d) Ananias, (e) angel. (19:11-12)

______ 6. As his shadow passed over invalids or tormented persons, they were healed. (a) Paul, (b) Peter, (c) Philip, (d) Ananias, (e) angel. (5:15-16)

______ 7. Appears in a vision to Gentile leader. (a) Paul, (b) Peter, (c) Philip, (d) Ananias, (e) angel. (10:1-8)

______ 8. Heals a beggar crippled from birth. (a) Paul, (b) Peter, (c) Philip, (d) Ananias, (e) angel. (3:2-8)

______ 9. Father of Malta estate owner Publius is healed. (a) Paul, (b) Peter, (c) Philip, (d) Ananias, (e) angel. (28:7-10)

______ 10. Helped Saul to receive both spiritual and physical eyesight. (a) Paul, (b) Peter, (c) Philip, (d) Ananias, (e) angel. (9:17-18)

______ 11. Dorcas (Tabitha) is raised from the dead. (a) Paul, (b) Peter, (c) Philip, (d) Ananias, (e) angel. (9:36-41)

______ 12. Eutychus is raised from the dead. (a) Paul, (b) Peter, (c) Philip, (d) Ananias, (e) angel. (20:9-12)

WORTHY OF SUFFERING

Solve the mystery of this verse by fitting one letter from each column into a square above the column. A dark square means the end of a word.

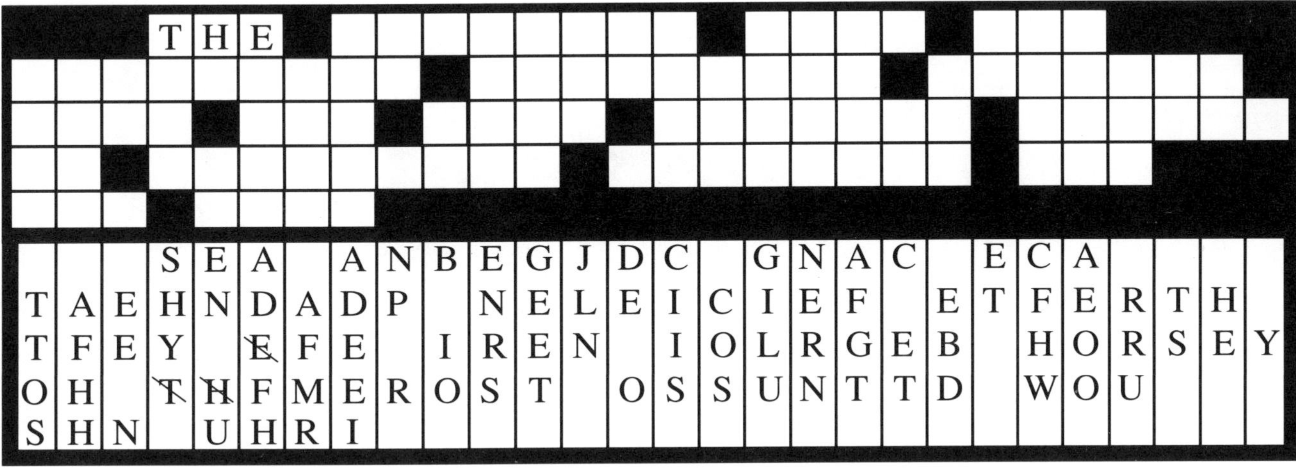

SLOWLY I TURN, STEP BY STEP
(Acts 13–16)

Below are two groups of events recorded in Acts. Put each group in correct order as recorded in Scripture.

I. CHAPTERS 13 AND 14 (Number 1 to 11)

_____ Paul and Barnabas report *back* to Antioch.

_____ Crowd calls Paul and Barnabas gods.

_____ Paul heals crippled man at Lystra.

_____ The team retraces their route, encouraging many along the way.

_____ Saul and Barnabas are sent as missionaries from Antioch.

_____ Confrontation of Paul and the sorcerer Elymas.

_____ Paul publicly declares the gospel for Gentiles too.

_____ Paul preaches at Pisidian Antioch.

_____ Crowd turns on Paul and stones him.

_____ Paul and Barnabas preach in Derbe.

_____ Many Jews and Gentiles become believers at Iconium.

II. CHAPTERS 15 AND 16 (Number 1 to 12)

_____ Midnight hymns and earthquake.

_____ Paul and Barnabas sent from Antioch to Jerusalem.

_____ Paul and Barnabas carry Council's letter to Antioch.

_____ Lydia, seller of purple cloth, converted.

_____ Apostles and elders gather to make decision.

_____ Paul and Barnabas disagree over John Mark; team splits.

_____ Philippian jailer and household converted.

_____ Timothy joins Paul and Silas at Lystra.

_____ Paul's vision of man from Macedonia.

_____ Paul and Silas imprisoned.

_____ Paul and Silas become missionary team.

_____ Council decides Gentiles are not bound to Jewish laws.

PAUL'S TRAVELOGUE

Paul took three missionary journeys and one final trip to Rome. Each trip was full of adventure as God worked through Paul and others involved. Below is an out-of-order list of happenings on those trips. On the line before each one, write 1, 2, 3, or F:

1 for first missionary journey (Acts 12:25 to 14:26)

2 for second missionary journey (Acts 15:36 to 18:22)

3 for third missionary journey (Acts 18:23 to 21:15)

F for final journey to Rome (Acts 27:1 to 28:31)

_______ 1. Paul preaches his message to the men of Athens.

_______ 2. Barnabas and John Mark accompany Paul.

_______ 3. The Corinthian church is established.

_______ 4. Paul declares the gospel is for the Gentiles also.

_______ 5. Stays at Malta for three months.

_______ 6. Idol maker, feeling his business threatened, creates a riot.

_______ 7. A proconsul on Cyprus is converted.

_______ 8. Timothy first becomes a part of the "gospel team."

_______ 9. Paul spends much time in Ephesus.

_______ 10. Paul is accompanied by Julius, a centurion.

_______ 11. Paul receives the call to go to Macedonia.

_______ 12. Saul becomes known as Paul.

_______ 13. Lydia, a business woman, is converted.

_______ 14. Paul is bitten by a snake, but suffers no ill effects.

_______ 15. Silas becomes Paul's traveling companion.

_______ 16. Paul and Silas are imprisoned at Philippi. The jailer is converted, and a church is established.

_______ 17. This journey precedes the Council at Jerusalem where important issues are settled.

_______ 18. Aprons and handkerchiefs touched by Paul cure the sick and cast out demons.

_______ 19. Paul and others are shipwrecked due to a terrible storm.

_______ 20. Paul meets Aquila and Priscilla.

_______ 21. Even though under house arrest, Paul preaches and ministers to those coming to him.

LATER ACTS
(Acts 17–20)

Below are two groups of events recorded in Acts. Put each group in correct order as recorded in Scripture.

I. CHAPTERS 17 AND 18 (Number 1 to 9)

______ The Lord tells Paul to stay in Corinth; not to fear—many Christians there.

______ Riot over Paul and Silas in Thessalonica.

______ Paul leaves Priscilla and Aquila at Ephesus.

______ Paul's sermon in Athens about the unknown God.

______ Paul meets Aquila and Priscilla in Corinth.

______ Paul returns to Antioch.

______ Synagogue ruler Crispus and his household become believers.

______ Priscilla and Aquila explain the way of God more fully to Apollos.

______ Many converts in Berea, but Paul has to flee.

II. CHAPTERS 19 AND 20 (Number 1 to 9)

______ Ephesian believers receive the Holy Spirit as Paul teaches.

______ Paul revives Eutychus, victim of a long sermon.

______ Paul bids farewell to Ephesian Christian leaders at Miletus.

______ Idol-maker Demetrius stirs up riot in Ephesus.

______ Paul leaves Ephesus, tours churches.

______ Scrolls burned as sorcerers accept the gospel.

______ Paul preaches past midnight at Troas.

______ Handkerchiefs and aprons touched by Paul have power for healing.

______ Seven sons of Sceva, a Jewish priest, attempt to cast out demons.

ENSEMBLE ACTING

Have you ever noticed the nationalities that heard the gospel in their own native language at Pentecost? Read Acts 2:1, 4-11 here:

"When the day of Pentecost came, they were all together in one place. . . . All of them were filled with the Holy Spirit and began to speak in other tongues as the Spirit enabled them. Now there were staying in Jerusalem God-fearing Jews from every nation under heaven. When they heard this sound, a crowd came together in bewilderment, because each one heard them speaking in his own language. Utterly amazed, they asked: "Are not all these men who are speaking *Galileans?* Then how is it that each of us hears them in his own native language? *Parthians, Medes* and *Elamites;* residents of *Mesopotamia, Judea,* and *Cappadocia, Pontus* and *Asia, Phrygia* and *Pamphylia, Egypt* and the parts of Libya near *Cyrene;* visitors from *Rome* (both Jews and converts to Judaism); *Cretans* and *Arabs*—we hear them declaring the wonders of God in our own tongues!"

In the wordfind below, circle all of the peoples and countries whose languages were heard at Pentecost. Find the words exactly as they are italicized in the verses above. Remember, they may be forward or backward.

```
P   L   A   N   M   C   R   E   T   A   N   S   G   A
H   P   U   A   E   R   G   E   S   L   N   A   N   S
R   A   A   G   S   U   O   A   G   A   E   S   E   T
Y   R   B   M   O   I   D   M   E   E   R   T   F   A
G   T   G   H   P   I   A   L   E   N   I   A   H   J
I   H   S   K   O   H   I   L   N   M   E   O   B   M
A   I   U   P   T   L   Y   Q   A   T   E   R   R   S
S   A   T   U   A   T   V   L   W   X   P   D   Y   A
Z   N   N   G   M   B   E   C   I   D   H   Y   E   C
E   S   O   F   I   J   U   D   E   A   G   J   G   S
C   A   P   P   A   D   O   C   I   A   L   K   I   E
```

HIGH DRAMA, SUPERNATURAL POWER

Match person and event. (Some are used more than once.)

_____ 1. Scales dropped from his eyes. (9:18)

_____ 2. Whisked away from a newly born-again Ethiopian eunuch. (8:39)

_____ 3. Bitten by viper, no ill effects. (28:3-6)

_____ 4. Fell out window during long sermon; raised from the dead by Paul (20:9-12)

_____ 5. Chained to soldiers in prison asleep, an angel releases him. (12:6, 7)

_____ 6. Struck by a light from heaven; meets Jesus. (9:3-9)

_____ 7. Peter raised her from the dead. (9:36-42)

_____ 8. Prison singing and praying—earthquake, conversions. (16:24-40)

_____ 9. Through a vision, the Lord sends him to a well-known Pharisee. (9:10-11)

_____ 10. In a vision he sees what is clean and what isn't. (10:9-20)

_____ 11. A Macedonian vision—gospel is wanted. (16:9-10)

a. Dorcas (Tabitha)

b. Eutychus

c. Ananias

d. Saul

e. Paul

f. Peter

g. Silas

h. Philip

THE OLD TESTAMENT
IN ACTS

The apostles quoted Old Testament prophecy to show how Jesus was the fulfillment of it. Have you ever gone through the book of Acts to see how many quotations and references are made to Old Testament characters, happenings, and prophecy? It's an interesting study.

This example is given to you in cryptoverse form. Solve by replacing each letter with another. Two clues are given to help you: **B** is really **Y**, and **C** is actually **P.**

" 'AS DQO UEID HEBI, TYH IEBI, A GAUU CYNV

YND XB ICAVAD YS EUU COYCUO. BYNV IYSI ESH

HENTQDOVI GAUU CVYCQOIB, BYNV BYNST XOS

GAUU IOO PAIAYSI, BYNV YUH XOS GAUU HVOEX

HVOEXI. OPOS YS XB IOVPESDI, JYDQ XOS ESH

GYXOS, A GAUU CYNV YND XB ICAVAD AS DQYIO

HEBI, ESH DQOB GAUU CVYCQOIB.' "

FROM THE TOP

Below are groups of numbers representing words of a Bible verse. From the telephone, choose a letter to correspond to the number in the puzzle. To help you, a few correct letters are in place. Remember, a *2* might mean an *a, b,* or *c,* and so forth.

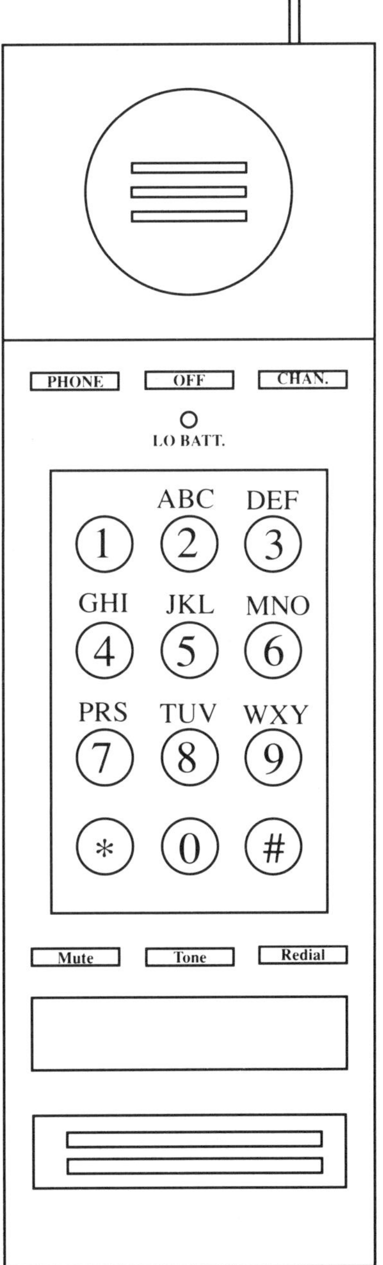

```
            c       i  e d        i   e r
 "8 4 3     2 4 7 2 8 6 2 4 7 3 3    2 3 5 4 3 8 3 7 7

                              e
 9 4 6    4 2 3    2 6 6 3    9 4 8 4    7 3 8 3 7

            o n   h
 9 3 7 3    2 7 8 6 6 4 7 4 3 3    8 4 2 8    8 4 3

                              p   r
 4 4 3 8    6 3    8 4 3    4 6 5 9    7 7 4 7 4 8    4 2 3

            p       d
 2 3 3 6    7 6 8 7 3 3    6 8 8    3 8 3 6    6 6

            G       e
 8 4 3    4 3 6 8 4 5 3 7."    — 2 2 8 7    * 10:H J
```

* Means Actual Number

IT HAPPENED HERE IN ACTS

CLUES ACROSS

1. Where Paul had Ephesian elders come to him in a sad farewell. (20:15-36)
4. Island where Paul confronted Bar-Jesus, a Jewish sorcerer and false prophet. (13:4-12)
6. City where Lydia responded to the gospel preached by Paul. (16:11-15)
9. Where Paul escapes the mob, but not Jason, his host. (17:1-9)
11. Where Saul was living when Barnabas sought him out to help in ministry at Antioch. (11:25)
13. Where Paul had the vision of the man from Macedonia asking for help. (16:8-10)
14. Where Paul appeared in the courts of Festus and Felix. (ch. 24–26)

15. Island where Paul and shipwreck victims took refuge. (28:1-10)
18. Philip was on the road from Jerusalem to __?__ when he met an Ethiopian eunuch. (8:26-27)
19. Saul was on this road to __?__ when he was confronted by Jesus Christ. (9:1-5)
21. Where Mark had deserted Paul and Barnabas. (15:37-38)
22. City that worshiped so many gods, Paul told them about the one and only God. (17:15-34)
23. Where Barnabas, Paul, Judas, and Silas delivered the Council's decision regarding the Law and Gentile believers. (15:22-30)
24. Where Paul spent the last few years of his life, preaching under guard. (28:11-31)

CLUES DOWN

1. Where Jesus was when He ascended to heaven. (1:9-12)
2. Paul had a fruitful ministry at this place, staying for three years. (19)
3. City where Peter raised Dorcas (Tabitha) from the dead. (9:36-42)
4. Where Paul stayed and worked with Aquila and Priscilla a year and a half. (18:1-11)
5. Where Paul and Barnabas saw many victories, then persecution and expulsion. (13:13-52)
7. City where the sticky question regarding the law and the Gentiles was decided. (ch. 15)
8. Where Paul was stoned, dragged out of city, and was thought to be dead. (14:8-20)
10. Temple gate where Peter and John met a crippled beggar. (Acts 3:1-2)
12. Where many accepted truth from Paul eagerly—examining the Scriptures daily. (17:10-12)
16. Jesus promised that after the power through the Holy Spirit came upon His people, they would witness of Him in Jerusalem, all Judea and __?__, and over the whole earth. (1:8)
17. Where Peter visited the saints and healed Aeneas. (9:32-35)
20. Island where prisoner Paul's ship sought unsuccessfully to winter. (27:7-44)

CLOSING ACTS
(Acts 21–28)

Put each of the two groups of events from Acts in correct order, as recorded in Scripture.

I. CHAPTERS 21 THROUGH 24 (Number 1 to 8)

_______ Paul uses Roman citizenship for defense.

_______ Plot uncovered; Paul secretly transported to Caesarea at night.

_______ Paul finished third missionary journey, and goes to Jerusalem.

_______ Paul appears before the Sanhedrin.

_______ Paul imprisoned for two years.

_______ Paul testifies to crowd in Aramaic.

_______ Trial before Felix.

_______ Paul seized by angry mob.

II. CHAPTERS 25 THROUGH 28 (Number 1 to 9)

_______ Prisoner Paul preaches Jesus to Roman Jews.

_______ Paul and others on island of Malta.

_______ Prisoner Paul sails toward Rome from Caesarea.

_______ Snake bites Paul; Paul unharmed.

_______ Arrives in Rome; under house arrest.

_______ Paul testifies before Agrippa and Bernice.

_______ Storm, then shipwrecked.

_______ Paul's trial before Festus.

_______ Paul heals; many gifts given in return.

NOMINEES FOR BEST ACTRESS

Match subjects to predicates.

_____ 1. Mary, mother of Jesus (1:14)

_____ 2. Bernice (25:13)

_____ 3. Priscilla (18:2, 3)

_____ 4. Lydia (16:14-15)

_____ 5. Damaris (17:34; 18:1)

_____ 6. Dorcas (9:36-39)

_____ 7. Candace (8:27)

_____ 8. Rhoda (12:13)

_____ 9. Mary, mother of John Mark (12:12)

_____ 10. Slave girl from Philippi (16:16-19)

a. converted at Athens.

b. answered door; found prison escapee.

c. visited Felix with King Agrippa.

d. used her home for a prayer meeting.

e. a lady, full of good deeds, died.

f. joined apostles and others in the Upper Room for prayer.

g. purple cloth dealer converted under Paul.

h. was a tentmaker, missionary.

i. a fortune-teller before demon cast out.

j. was queen of Ethiopia.

NOMINEES
FOR BEST DIALOGUE

Each quotation is taken from the *New International Version* of the Bible. Below there are four sets of answer choices, one set per question. The questions begin on the next page.

"WHO SAID IT?" CHOICES:
(Some will be repeated.)

a. evil spirit

b. Gamaliel

c. Jesus

d. the Lord

e. Paul

f. Peter

g. Peter and John

h. Peter and other apostles

i. Stephen

"WHERE WAS IT SAID?" CHOICES:
(One is used twice, one—3 times.)

<. Caesarea

=. Corinth

#. Damascus

$. Ephesus

%. Miletus

@ Mount of Olives

&. outside Jerusalem

*. assembly of Sanhedrin in temple

+. temple gate called Beautiful

"TO WHOM WAS IT SAID?" CHOICES:
(One is used three times.)

A. Ananias

B. apostles

C. Cornelius

D. elders of Ephesian church

E. to the Lord

F. his friends

G. beggar crippled from birth

H. high priest and Israel's elders

I. Paul

J. 7 sons of Sceva, a chief priest

CHAPTER IN ACTS—CHOICES:

1

3

4

5

5

7

9

10

18

19

20

21

1. "Therefore, in the present case I advise you: Leave these men alone! Let them go! For if their purpose or activity is of human origin, it will fail. But if it is from God, you will not be able to stop these men; you will only find yourselves fighting against God."

_______ Who said it? v. 34

_______ To whom was it said? vv. 21, 34

_______ Where was it said? v. 27

_______ Chapter in Acts?

2. Then ——— answered, "Why are you weeping and breaking my heart? I am ready not only to be bound, but also to die in Jerusalem for the name of the Lord Jesus."

_______ Who said it? v. 13

_______ To whom was it said? vv. 8-14

_______ Where was it said? v. 8

_______ Chapter in Acts?

3. Then ——— said, "Silver or gold I do not have, but what I have I give you. In the name of Jesus Christ of Nazareth, walk."

_______ Who said it? v. 6

_______ To whom was it said? v. 2

_______ Where was it said? v. 2

_______ Chapter in Acts?

4. "But you will receive power when the Holy Spirit comes on you; and you will be my witnesses in Jerusalem, and in all Judea and Samaria, and to the ends of the earth."

_______ Who said it? v. 1

_______ To whom was it said? v. 2

_______ Where was it said? v. 12

_______ Chapter in Acts?

5. Then he fell on his knees and cried out, "————, do not hold this sin against them."

_______ Who said it? v. 59

_______ To whom was it said? v. 60

_______ Where was it said? v. 58

_______ Chapter in Acts?

6. But ——— said to ———, "Go! This man is my chosen instrument to carry my name before the Gentiles and their kings and before the people of Israel. I will show him how much he must suffer for my name."

_______ Who said it? v. 15

_______ To whom was it said? v. 15

_______ Where was it said? v. 10

_______ Chapter in Acts?

7. "However, I consider my life worth nothing to me, if only I may finish the race and complete the task the Lord Jesus has given me—the task of testifying to the gospel of God's grace."

_______ Who said it? vv. 17-18

_______ To whom was it said? vv. 17-18

....

______ Where was it said? v. 17

______ Chapter in Acts?

8. ——— and ——— apostles replied: "We must obey God rather than men!"

______ Who said it? v. 29

______ To whom was it said? v. 27

______ Where was it said? v. 27

______ Chapter in Acts?

9. Then ——— began to speak: "I now realize how true it is that God does not show favoritism but accepts men from every nation who fear him and do what is right."

______ Who said it? v. 34

______ To whom was it said? vv. 30-34

______ Where was it said? v. 24

______ Chapter in Acts?

10. One day the evil spirit answered them, "Jesus I know, and I know about Paul, but who are you?"

______ Who said it? v. 15

______ To whom was it said? v. 14

______ Where was it said? v. 17

______ Chapter in Acts?

11. But ——— and ——— replied, "Judge for yourselves whether it is right in God's sight to obey you rather than God. For we cannot help speaking about what we have seen and heard."

______ Who said it? v. 19

______ To whom was it said? vv. 15, 18

______ Where was it said? vv. 15, 18

______ Chapter in Acts?

12. One night ——— spoke to ——— in a vision: "Do not be afraid; keep on speaking, do not be silent. For I am with you, and no one is going to attack and harm you, because I have many people in this city."

______ Who said it? v. 9

______ To whom was it said? v. 9

______ Where was it said? vv. 1, 8

______ Chapter in Acts?

....

NOMINEES FOR BEST ACTOR, PETER OR PAUL?

Each statement refers to something Peter or Paul or both did. Write the appropriate answer on the line before the number.

_______ 1. Who also had another name recorded in Scripture?

_______ 2. Who healed a beggar at the Temple Gate?

_______ 3. Who preached in Athens?

_______ 4. Who testified before Herod Agrippa?

_______ 5. Who considered Timothy his son in the Lord?

_______ 6. Who was imprisoned and miraculously released?

_______ 7. Who raised someone from the dead?

_______ 8. Who received the Holy Spirit at Pentecost?

_______ 9. Who was friend and coworker with Aquila and Priscilla?

_______ 10. Who spoke at the Jerusalem Council?

_______ 11. Who first took the gospel to the Gentiles?

_______ 12. Who shook off a snake into the fire?

_______ 13. Who was the "Apostle to the Gentiles"?

_______ 14. Who preached a sermon and 3,000 were converted?

_______ 15. Who had been a member of the Sanhedrin?

HELPFUL SCRIPTURES: (1) Acts 13:9; 2 Peter 1:1. (2) Acts 3:2-10. (3) Acts 17:16-31. (4) Acts 25:23–26:32. (5) 1 Timothy 1:1, 2, 18; 2 Timothy 1:2. (6) Acts 5:18-29; 12:5-10; 16:22-33. (7) Acts 9:40, 41; 20:7-12. (8) Acts 1:13–2:14. (9) Acts 18:1-3. (10) Acts 15:2-12. (11) Acts 10:23-46. (12) Acts 28:4, 5. (13) Acts 9:11-15; 14:23-27; 22:21, 22. (14) Acts 2:14-41. (15) Acts 9:1, 2; 22:2-5; 23:1, 6.

NOMINEES FOR BEST FOREIGN LANGUAGE

Our world had one language before the Tower of Babel confusion. It remained confused through history until the day of Pentecost. Acts 2:5-6 tells us, "Now there were staying in Jerusalem God-fearing Jews from every nation under heaven. When they heard this sound, a crowd came together in bewilderment, because each one heard them speaking in his own language."

One can only imagine the great joy of hearing "the wonders of God in our own tongues" (2:11) when diversity of language prevails.

At that moment the fulfillment of Jesus' words in Acts 1:8 had begun, "But you will receive power when the Holy Spirit comes on you; and you will be my witnesses in Jerusalem, and in all Judea and Samaria, and to the ends of the earth."

What if God's Word was unavailable in English? Imagining that is mind-boggling. The work of translating Scripture both historically and today around the world is life-giving. Today's translators and missionaries tell exciting stories about people of other tongues learning that God speaks their language too.

Below I have collected Acts 1:8 in several languages. See how many you can match.

______ 1. Recibireis, sí, la virtud del Espíritu Santo que descenderá sobre vosotros, y me serviréis de testigos en Jerusalén, y en toda la Judea, y Samaria, y hasta el cabo del mundo.
  —Hechos De Los Apóstoles

______ 2. Icyakora muzahabg' imbaraga, Umwuka Wera n' abamanukira; kandi muzab' abagabo bo kumpamya, i Yerusalemu n'i Yudaya yose n'i Samaria no kugeza ku mpera y' isi.
  —Ivyakozwe n' Intumwa

______ 3. "Men ni skall få kraft när den heliga anden kommer över er, och ni skall vittna om mig i Jerusalem och i hela Judeen och Samarien och ända till jordens yttersta gräns."
  —Apostlagärningarna

a. French

b. Swedish

c. Hebrew

d. Ancient Greek

e. Spanish

f. Modern Greek

g. Kinyarwanda (Rwanda, Africa)

_______ 4. Sondern ihr werdet die Kraft des Heiligen Geistes empfangen, welcher auf euch Kommen wird, und werdet meine Zeugen Sein zu Jerusalem und in ganz Judäa und Samarien und bis an das Ende der Erde.
  —Apostelgeschichte

_______ 5. ἀλλὰ θὰ λάβετε δύναμιν, ὅταν ἔλθῃ τὸ "Αγιον Πνεῦμα ἐπάνω σας, καὶ θὰ εἰσθε μάρτυρές μου εἰς την Ιερουσαλημ καὶ εἰς ὁλόκληρη την Ἰουδαίαν καὶ Σαμάρειαν καὶ μέχρι τῶν περάτων τῆς γῆς.
  —ΠΡΑΞΕΙΣ ΑΠΟΣΤΟΛΩΝ

_______ 6. ἀλλὰ λήμψεσθε δύναμιν ἐπελθόντος τοῦ ἁγίου πνεύματος ἐφ' υμᾶς καὶ εσεσθέ μου μάρτυρες εν τε Ἰερουσαλήμ καὶ °[εν] πάσῃ τῃ Ἰουδαίᾳ καὶ Σαμαρεια καὶ εως ἐσχάτου τῆς γῆς.
  —(ΠΡΑΞΕΙΣ ΑΠΟΣΤΟΛΩΝ)

_______ 7. Mais vous recevrez une puissance, le Saint-Esprit survenant sur vous, et vous serez mes témoins à Jérusalem, dans toute la Judée, dans la Samarie, et jusqu'aux etrémités de la terre.
  —ACTES DES APÔTRES

_______ 8. אֲבָל תְּקַבְּלוּ גְבוּרָה בְּבוֹא עֲלֵיכֶם רוּחַ הַקֹּדֶשׁ

וִהְיִיתֶם עֵדַי בִּירוּשָׁלַיִם וּבְכָל־יְהוּדָה

וּבְשֹׁמְרוֹן וְעַד־קְצֵה הָאָרֶץ׃

ANSWERS TO ALL PUZZLES AND QUIZZES

ANSWERS TO "CAST OF CHARACTERS":
1. ANANIAS, 2. PETER, 3. BARNABAS, 4. JOHN MARK, 5. SILAS, 6. TIMOTHY, 7. AQUILA & PRISCILLA, 8. CRISPUS, 9. APOLLOS, 10. DEMETRIUS, 11. EUTYCHUS, 12. AGABUS, 13. HEROD, 14. FELIX, 15. AGRIPPA.

ANSWERS TO "SETTING THE SCENE":
1. l; 2. g; 3. d; 4. k; 5. e; 6. b; 7. h; 8. a; 9. i; 10. f; 11. c; 12. j

ANSWERS TO "OPENING ACTS" (ACTS 1–4):
I. 2, 5, 4, 3, 9, 8, 6, 10, 7, 1
II. 6, 4, 7, 3, 5, 2, 1

ANSWERS TO "WHO ACTED THIS WAY?":
1. PETER, JOHN 2. ANANIAS, SAPPHIRA 3. GAMALIEL 4. PHILIP 5. JESUS 6. STEPHEN 7. SIMON the SORCERER 8. SAUL 9. ETHIOPIAN EUNUCH 10. MATTHIAS 11. CORNELIUS 12. BARNABAS 13. DORCAS 14. JAMES 15. LUKE.

ANSWERS TO "SCENE CHANGES":
1. d; 2. e; 3. k; 4. i; 5. a; 6. b; 7. j; 8. c; 9. g; 10. f; 11. h.

ANSWERS TO "WHAT COMES NEXT?":
I. 7, 10, 1, 2, 5, 9, 4, 6, 8, 3
II. 9, 3, 1, 7, 12, 4, 6, 8, 5, 10, 2, 11

ANSWERS TO "KEEPING THE CHARACTERS STRAIGHT" (FIRST PART):

PEOPLE BY NAME

Annas	Bernice
Andrew	Caiaph
Caesar	Cornelius
Crispus	Sergius Paulus
Drusilla	Elymas
Demetrius	Dionysius
Erastus	Gallio
Gamaliel	Judas
James	John
Claudius Lysias	Simon
James	Manaen
Judas	Lydia
Joseph	Nicanor
Mary	John Mark
Nicolas	Lucius
Philip	Secundus
Publius	Simeon
Simon	Timon
Titius Justus	Procorus
Tychicus	Trophimus
Tertullus	

PEOPLE BY OCCUPATION

captain of temple guard
slave girl, fortune-teller
crippled beggar
Philippian jailer
centurions
commander
magistrate
sentries
soldiers
chief priests

O.T. MEN MENTIONED

Isaiah	Abraham
Joshua	Moses
Aaron	David
Isaac	Joel
Jacob	

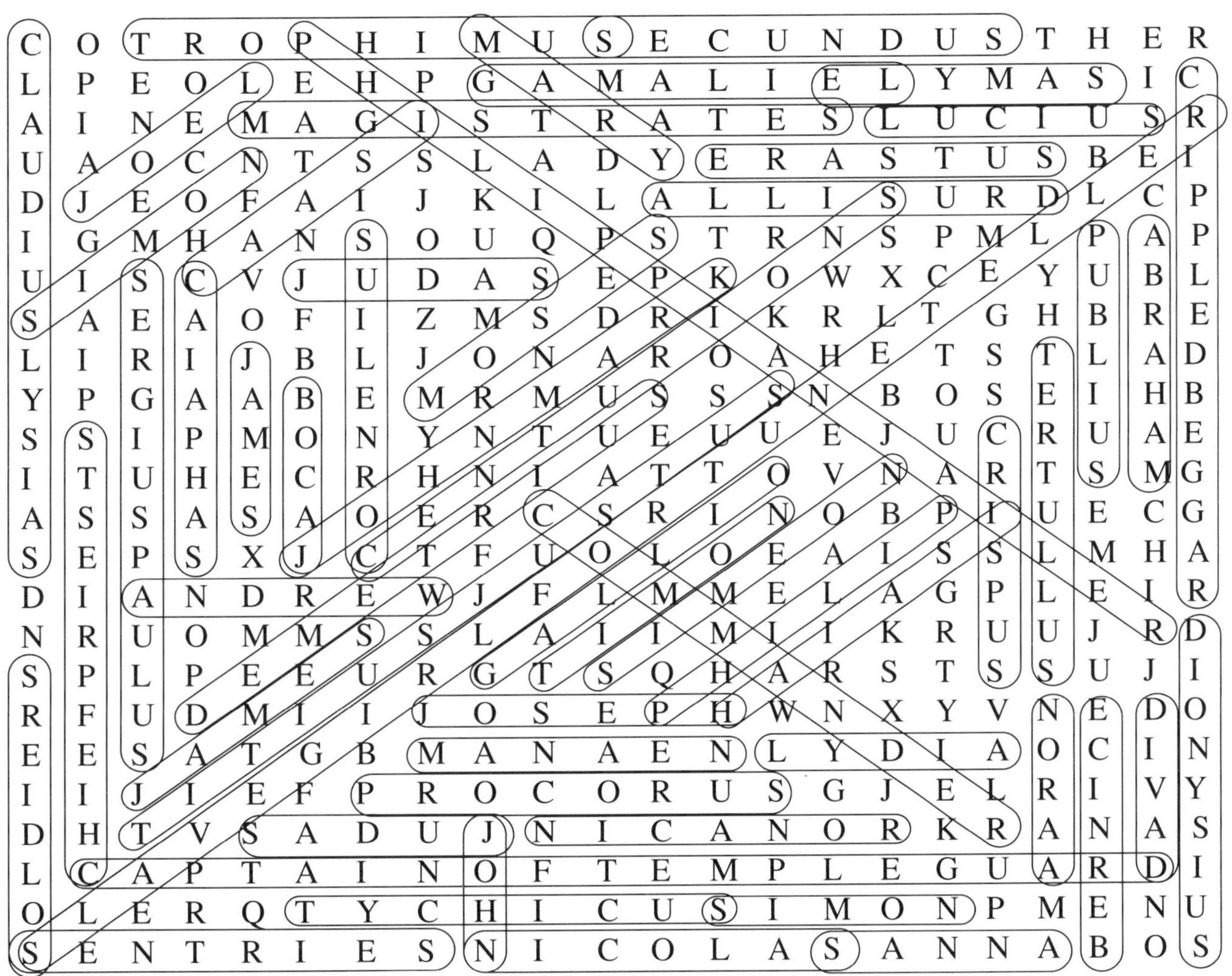

ANSWERS TO "HOLY SPIRIT SPECIAL EFFECTS":

A. 3, 18, 26, 32, 42, 52, 61, 72, 86, 89, 90, 96

B. 1, 12, 28, 31, 41, 51, 64, 71, 85, 87, 88

C. 1, 13, 25, 34, 41, 51, 62, 71, 91, 92

D. 5, 11, 24, 36, 62, 71, 95, 90, 93

E. 6, 15, 21, 36, 61, 72, 94, 83, 90

F. 4, 17, 23, 34, 62, 72, 82

ANSWERS TO "KNOW YOUR SCRIPT":

1) 9, 2) 6, 3) 1, 4) 3, 5) 2, 6) 11, 7) 13–14, 8) 1, 9) 2, 10) 9, 11) 7, 12) 8, 13) 5, 12, 14) 10, 15) 7 (v. 58), 16) 5.

ANSWERS TO "FOLLOW YOUR SCRIPT, PLEASE":

1) 28, 2) 18, 3) 27, 4) 18–21, 5) 15, 6) 21, 7) 18, 8) 15–18, 9) 16, 10) 16, 11) 24, 12) 28, 13) 25, 14) 25, 26, 15) 16.

ANSWERS TO "CROSSING THE STAGE":

ACROSS	*DOWN*
4. Pilate	1. Bartholomew
6. Felix	2. Mary
8. Agabus	3. Judas
9. Sosthenes	4. Peter
11. Aeneas	5. Timothy
13. cut	6. Festus
15. help	7. Joseph
16. language	9. Stephen
18. Rhoda	10. Eutychus
20. Matthew	12. Sceva
22. Jason	14. gate
24. Gaius	17. Blastus
25. eunuch	19. Apollos
26. Jesus	21. Theophilus
27. Paul	23. Saul
28. Sopater	26. John
29. Ananias	27. Priscilla
31. serious	28. Sapphira
32. Philip	29. Aristarchus

34. Agrippa
35. Dorcas
36. hour
37. God
39. Matthias
41. jail
43. Alexander
46. Amen
47. Candace
48. Thomas
49. resist
50. Trophimus
51. lived
52. Damaris

30. Simon
33. Parmenas
38. Barnabas
40. Silas
42. Aquila
44. angel
45. Herod

....

ANSWERS TO "THE PLOT THICKENS":

I. 6, 12, 2, 3, 1, 9, 7, 10, 4, 11, 13, 5, 8

II. 3, 1, 8, 9, 7, 4, 6, 2, 5

ANSWERS TO "MODUS OPERANDI":

1. a; 2. b; 3. c; 4. a; 5. a; 6. b; 7. e; 8. b; 9. a; 10. d; 11. b; 12. a

ANSWER TO "WORTHY OF SUFFERING":

Acts 5:41 "The apostles left the Sanhedrin, rejoicing because they had been counted worthy of suffering disgrace for the Name."

ANSWERS TO "SLOWLY I TURN, STEP BY STEP":

I. 11, 7, 6, 10, 1, 2, 4, 3, 8, 9, 5

II. 11, 1, 4, 9, 2, 5, 12, 7, 8, 10, 6, 3

ANSWERS TO "PAUL'S TRAVELOGUE":

1. 2	Acts 17:19-31		12. 1	Acts 13:9
2. 1	12:25		13. 2	16:14
3. 2	18:1-11		14. F	28:3-6
4. 1	13:46-48		15. 2	15:40
5. F	28:1, 11		16. 2	16:22-34
6. 3	19:23-29		17. 1	14:26 to 15:1-30
7. 1	13:4-12		18. 3	19:11-12
8. 2	16:1-3		19. F	27:14-44
9. 3	19		20. 2	18:2
10. F	27:1		21. F	28:30-31
11. 2	16:9			

ANSWERS TO "LATER ACTS":

I. 6, 1, 7, 3, 4, 8, 5, 9, 2

II. 1, 8, 9, 5, 6, 4, 7, 2, 3

....

ANSWER TO "ENSEMBLE ACTING":

```
P  L  A  N  M  C  R  E  T  A  N  S  G  A
H  P  U  A  E  R  G  E  S  L  N  A  N  S
R  A  A  G  S  U  O  A  G  A  E  S  E  T
Y  R  B  M  O  I  D  M  E  E  R  T  F  A
G  T  G  H  P  I  A  L  E  N  I  A  H  J
I  H  S  K  O  H  I  L  N  M  E  O  B  M
A  I  U  P  T  L  Y  Q  A  T  E  R  R  S
S  A  T  U  A  T  V  L  W  X  P  D  Y  A
Z  N  N  G  M  B  E  C  I  D  H  Y  E  C
E  S  O  F  I  J  U  D  E  A  G  J  G  S
C  A  P  P  A  D  O  C  I  A  L  K  I  E
```

ANSWERS TO "HIGH DRAMA, SUPERNATURAL POWER":

1. d; 2. h; 3. e; 4. b; 5. f; 6. d; 7. a; 8. e, g; 9. c; 10. f; 11. e.

ANSWER TO "THE OLD TESTAMENT IN ACTS":

Acts 2:17-18: " 'In the last days, God says, I will pour out my Spirit on all people. Your sons and daughters will prophesy, your young men will see visions, your old men will dream dreams. Even on my servants, both men and women, I will pour out my Spirit in those days, and they will prophesy.' "

ANSWER TO "FROM THE TOP":

Acts 10:45 "The circumcised believers who had come with Peter were astonished that the gift of the Holy Spirit had been poured out even on the Gentiles."

ANSWERS TO "IT HAPPENED HERE IN ACTS":

ACROSS

1. Miletus
4. Cyprus
6. Philippi
9. Thessalonica
11. Tarsus
13. Troas
14. Caesarea
15. Malta
18. Gaza
19. Damascus
21. Pamphylia
22. Athens
23. Antioch
24. Rome

DOWN

1. Mount of Olives
2. Ephesus
3. Joppa
4. Corinth
5. Pisidian Antioch
7. Jerusalem
8. Lystra
10. Beautiful
12. Berea
16. Samaria
17. Lydda
20. Crete

ANSWERS TO "CLOSING ACTS":
I. 4, 6, 1, 5, 8, 3, 7, 2
II. 9, 5, 3, 6, 8, 2, 4, 1, 7

ANSWERS TO "NOMINEES FOR BEST ACTRESS":
 1. f
 2. c
 3. h
 4. g
 5. a
 6. e
 7. j
 8. b
 9. d
10. i

ANSWERS TO "NOMINEES FOR BEST DIALOGUE":
 1. b, H, *, 5
 2. e, F, <, 21
 3. f, G, +, 3
 4. c, B, @, 1
 5. i, E, &, 7
 6. d or c, A, #, 9
 7. e, D, %, 20
 8. h, H, *, 5
 9. f, C, <, 10
10. a, J, $, 19
11. g, H, *, 4
12. d or c, I, =, 18

ANSWERS TO "NOMINEES FOR BEST ACTOR, PETER OR PAUL?":
I. Both 2. Peter 3. Paul 4. Paul 5. Paul 6. Both 7. Both 8. Peter 9. Paul 10. Both
II. Peter 12. Paul 13. Paul 14. Peter 15. Paul

ANSWERS TO "NOMINEES FOR BEST FOREIGN LANGUAGE":
1. e 2. g 3. b 4. h 5. f 6. d 7. a 8. c